Virtues in Action

Empowering Kids and Families to Connect, Grow, and Thrive

BOOK ONE

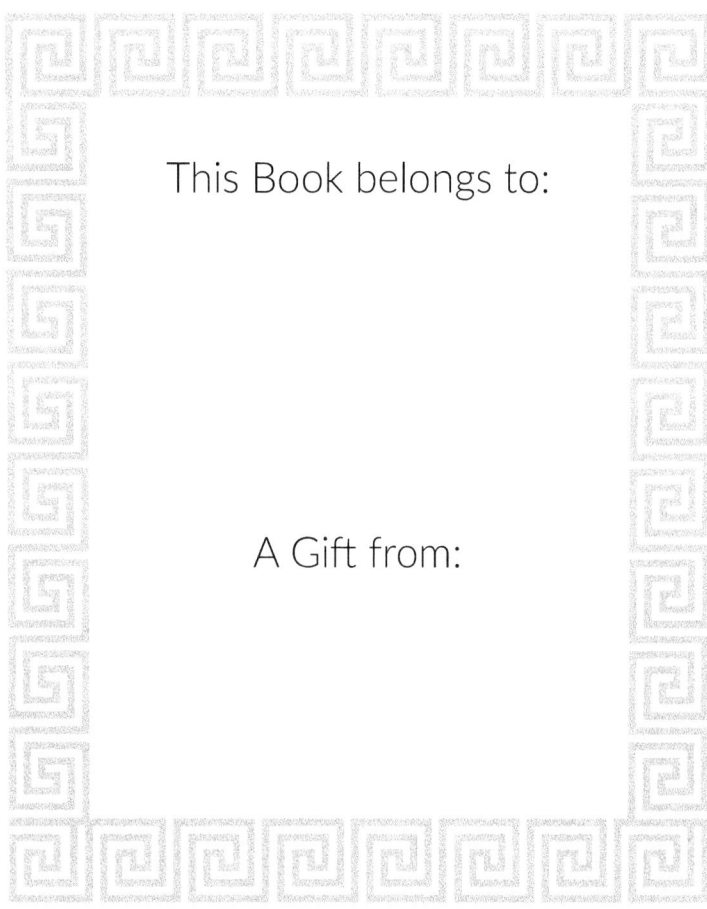

This Book belongs to:

A Gift from:

© 2011-2025 ThinkVirtues LLC, Kathy Motlagh - All rights reserved.

ISBN 978-0-9849950-7-3

This book and the accompanying illustrations are protected under copyright law. No part of this publication may be reproduced, stored in a retrieval system, or transmitted in any form or by any means—electronic, mechanical, photocopying, recording, or otherwise—without the prior written permission of the copyright owner, except in the case of brief quotations embodied in critical articles or reviews.

For permissions, please contact info@thinkvirtues.com

INTRODUCTION

Congratulations on making a meaningful investment in your child's well-being and future success. This book is a gateway to fostering your child's social-emotional learning, cultivating strong character, and helping them discover the incredible power they hold within.

Through the lessons and exercises in this book, your child will learn how to navigate negative emotions, embrace positivity, and make decisions that truly serve them. They'll gain the tools to choose friends who are kind, respectful, and loving, and to build a hopeful, empowered perspective on themselves and their future.

None of us are born with the skills for happiness or success—these are qualities we learn, nurture, and refine through practice. This journey toward greatness is a shared path, and by engaging in the thoughtful conversations and activities in this book, you'll be supporting your child in developing these life-changing traits.

To deepen this journey, we also offer *Virtues Cards for Kids* and *Virtues Cards for Adults*. These tools can enrich your experience and help you and your family continue to grow in wisdom and strength.

The great minds of history—Socrates, Aristotle, Plato, and many others—taught us that the foundation of a happy, successful life is the practice of virtues. By embracing this opportunity, you are giving your child the gift of a strong character and a life filled with joy and purpose.

With love and gratitude for the journey ahead,

ThinkVirtues®

TO THE TRAVELER ON THIS JOURNEY INTO JOY

Welcome to Your Journey of Self-Discovery, Growth, and Empowerment!

You hold an incredible power within you—the power to become whoever you choose to be. This workbook is your companion on the path to becoming the best version of yourself. It's designed to equip you with the tools to bring more joy, enthusiasm, and success into every area of your life.

Within you lies untapped potential, waiting to be uncovered. Together, let's explore the virtues you already possess and learn how to harness them for achievement and fulfillment. By doing so, you'll not only uplift yourself but also inspire positivity and power in those around you. Virtues are your superpowers—let's discover how to activate them!

Here's how to make the most of this book:

1. **Understanding the Virtue:**
   At the beginning of each focus on a new virtue, take a moment to read its description. Reflect on what this virtue means to you. Use the journal section to write how it helps you connect with others, achieve success, or navigate challenges.

2. **The Importance of the Virtue:**
   Explore why this virtue matters. In the journaling space, delve deeper into its significance in your life and how it can shape your relationships, goals, and growth.

3. **Visualization Practice:**
   Set aside time to visualize yourself embodying the virtue. Find a quiet space, relax, and imagine yourself practicing and living this virtue. How does it feel? Does it bring a sense of confidence, peace, or power?

4. **Expanding Your Knowledge:**
   Discover recommended readings to deepen your understanding of each virtue. Dive into these resources and let them inspire new insights and ideas.

5. **Creative Expression:**
   Engage your creativity through exercises and activities in this section. Don't stop there—think of additional ways to express the virtue and jot them down in your journal.

6. **Family Connection:**
   Bring your family into the journey! Explore the family activity section and share experiences together. Use the prompts to reflect on what you learned and how it felt to practice the virtue as a team.

7. **Self-Reflection:**
   Take time to evaluate your experience with each virtue. At first, it may feel unfamiliar or even challenging, but with practice, you'll find yourself naturally incorporating it into your daily life. Reflect on how this growth makes you feel and the positive changes it brings.

8. **Journaling Your Progress:**
   The journaling section is a safe space for you to document your thoughts and feelings. How did this month's virtue impact your happiness, confidence, or hopefulness? Write about the outcomes and how practicing the virtue influenced your day-to-day activities.

Enjoy every step of this transformative journey. We also offer additional tools, like Virtues Cards for Kids and Adults, to deepen your engagement with these timeless principles and support your continued growth.

Here's to discovering your greatness and living a life of empowerment and joy!

BOOK ONE

Assertiveness   1

Flexibility   21

Forgiveness   41

Generosity   61

Joyfulness   85

Love   107

Patience   131

Respect   155

Thankfulness   179

This is Book One in a Six-Book Series by ThinkVirtues®
Find more Books and the Master Collection of Virtues
at ThinkVirtues.com

Thoughts become words. Words become action. Actions become character. Character becomes destiny.
©2024 ThinkVirtues, LLC. All Rights Reserved.

Assertiveness

FOCUS 1

The Meaning of Assertiveness

Assertiveness is being confident and self-assured enough to stand up for what you believe in and being able to express your thoughts, feelings, beliefs, wants, or needs without denying or ignoring the thoughts, feelings, beliefs, wants, or needs of others.

What are three ways you can practice Assertiveness?

1. _____

2. _____

3. _____

ThinkVirtues®

Assertiveness

FOCUS 2

The Importance of Assertiveness

The virtue of assertiveness helps ensure better, more positive communication in a mutually respectful relationship. Model practicing assertiveness to help your child learn how to counterbalance between aggressiveness and passivity when communicating. Practicing assertiveness helps your child build confidence in their self and their ability to work successfully with others in a win-win life strategy. This important virtue helps them stand up to someone instead of letting them be controlled — even independently when a parent or adult is not present.

Why is it important to practice Assertiveness?

_____

_____

_____

_____

_____

_____

ThinkVirtues®

Assertiveness

FOCUS 3

Visualizing and Meditating on Assertiveness

Imagine yourself accomplishing the ability to be assertive. Now focus on that goal and keep it in your mind as your child finds difficulties and distractions when achieving assertiveness. Remember that these distractions can be very appealing because of feeling mean. Imagine yourself being assertive in these situations. What would that look like? How would you feel? You may find it uncomfortable; people who are naturally more aggressive might not want to let go of the feeling they have of power, domination, or control over others.

How will you invite and deeply embrace the essence of Assertiveness?

_____

_____

_____

How do you feel after you have succeeded?

_____

_____

_____

ThinkVirtues®

FOCUS 3

Visualizing and Meditating on Assertiveness

How will you look or act being assertive?

_____

_____

_____

_____

_____

_____

_____

_____

ThinkVirtues®

Assertiveness

FOCUS 4

Here are some books you will enjoy reading!
They show assertiveness in the characters.
You can get these books from your local library or bookstore.

If you are 5 to 12 years old, you will enjoy reading:
The Juice Box Bully: Empowering Kids to Stand Up for Others
by Bob Sornson and Maria Dismondy

If you are 6 to 9 years old, you will enjoy reading:
The Streets are Free
by Kurusa

ThinkVirtues®

Assertiveness

FOCUS 4

ThinkVirtues®

Assertiveness

FOCUS 5

Let's be creative!

As a family, come up with a list of everyday occurrences where you can practice assertiveness.

_____

_____

_____

_____

_____

_____

_____

_____

ThinkVirtues®

Assertiveness

FOCUS 5

Let's be creative!

Make a piece of art showing you practicing assertiveness.

- **Write a story or drama**
- **Write a song or poetry**
- **Create a dance**
- **Make painting or drawing**
- **Create a collage**

You can use the space below or grab some fun materials.

Thoughts become words. Words become action. Actions become character. Character becomes destiny.
©2024 ThinkVirtues, LLC. All Rights Reserved.

Assertiveness

FOCUS 6

Family Activity

As a family, develop a list of basic rights, a Family Bill of Rights. These rights might include such things as being able to say "no" when it is appropriate; standing up for what you believe; being respected (and respectful).
Also as a family, discuss ways that will help support those rights in difficult situations. Listen to each other and find ways to help each family member be assertive.

Name all of the rights discussed as a family and why you picked them.

_____

_____

_____

_____

_____

_____

ThinkVirtues®

FOCUS 6

Develop a plan for ways to carry out and support these rights.

ThinkVirtues®

Assertiveness

FOCUS 7

Use this day to think about the times when you showed assertiveness in an interaction with family, friends, or colleagues. Assertiveness takes practice and careful reflection about your own behaviors. Take time each day to think about being assertive.

How did you succeed? How were you not comfortable being assertive?

_____

_____

_____

_____

_____

_____

_____

ThinkVirtues®

FOCUS 7

What people around you are you most comfortable being assertive with? Write them down.

_____

_____

_____

_____

_____

_____

_____

ThinkVirtues®

Assertiveness

REFLECTION

Use these pages to document your experience with being assertive.
How does it feel inside to imagine yourself asserting yourself and being your own self advocate.
If you are afraid and worried, it is completely normal. Write your worries here. If not, feel free write whatever occurs to you.

_____

_____

_____

_____

_____

_____

_____

ThinkVirtues®

Assertiveness

REFLECTION

Look at your notes about any self-doubt, and say to yourself out loud:
This is the way I used to be; I no longer have any self-doubt because I know I can become assertive by practicing it every day.
Then take the rest of the pages to express all the ways you would like to be assertive.

_____

_____

_____

_____

_____

_____

_____

_____

ThinkVirtues®

Assertiveness

REFLECTION

ThinkVirtues®

REFLECTION

Thoughts become words. Words become action. Actions become character. Character becomes destiny.
©2024 ThinkVirtues, LLC. All Rights Reserved.

ThinkVirtues®

Assertiveness

REFLECTION

ThinkVirtues®

Assertiveness

REFLECTION

Thoughts become words. Words become action. Actions become character. Character becomes destiny.

ThinkVirtues®

Thoughts become words. Words become action. Actions become character. Character becomes destiny.
©2024 ThinkVirtues, LLC. All Rights Reserved.

ThinkVirtues®

Flexibility

FOCUS 1

The Meaning of Flexibility

Flexibility means recognizing that things can change and then being willing and able to adjust to the changes. Flexibility is what many psychologists refer to as mental or emotional resilience. Rather than trying to control circumstances, the flexible person is pliable and adapts to make the best of the new situation. In the literal sense, flexibility means being able to bend without breaking; in the sense of the virtue, it means being able to adjust to something new without it "breaking" or harming the person.

You practice flexibility when you consider a situation in the context of recognizing that while it may be a very difficult or challenging time, things will get better. Further, being flexible calls for mentally practicing ideas that foster that understanding by being around people who also support that notion, looking for the positive in every situation, and recognizing that difficult, painful, or sad times are a normal part of life.

Instead of seeing all situations as black-and-white, or right or wrong, flexible people recognize that life is complex. Every life circumstance has both positive and negative aspects, and recognizing this helps a person develop a more flexible viewpoint in which both sides of the proverbial coin are examined and considered as having legitimate points to consider.

Flexibility implies change, so learning something new can help encourage flexible thinking. It doesn't matter what the learning experience is; it can be learning a musical instrument or how to dance, taking a class in writing or a new language, or developing your cooking skills. Any novel activity is a possibility as long as it is a new learning experience for you. Even changing your daily routine can help develop flexibility.

ThinkVirtues®

Flexibility

FOCUS 1

What are three ways you can practice Flexibility?

1. _____

2. _____

3. _____

ThinkVirtues®

Flexibility

FOCUS 2

The Importance of Flexibility

Life has its ups and downs. The image of a "perfect," problem-free existence is a myth! Recognizing and accepting that notion is an important first step in learning the necessity of flexibility.

Flexible people do well in a variety of situations, even being able to learn from negative times and see the positive in difficult times. The ability to adapt and make the best of things leads to greater peace and contentment overall. Rather than blaming other people or feeling cheated by life, flexible people are able to accept responsibility for how they respond to what happens to them.

Flexible people tend to be happier since they feel calmer and more in control of their lives. They often feel that they have mastered the negative times in a way that ultimately produces positive outcomes. Ironically, flexibility contributes to overall health and well-being just as healthy habits contribute to greater flexibility of thinking. Conversely, inflexibility can often be associated with greater instances of depression and difficulty in coping with unanticipated or painful life circumstances

Why is it important to practice Flexibility?

_____

_____

_____

ThinkVirtues®

Flexibility

FOCUS 2

The Importance of Flexibility

_____

_____

_____

_____

_____

_____

_____

_____

_____

ThinkVirtues®

Flexibility

FOCUS 3

Visualizing and Meditating on Flexibility

Close your eyes and think of a time when you reacted to a difficult or new situation with rigidity. You may have fallen back into an old habit or found yourself wanting to change the situation or the people involved instead of adjusting your own thinking or reactions. What was the outcome for you? What was it for the other person(s) involved? How satisfied were you with the resolution to the problem?

Now imagine yourself being more flexible in that same situation. What would you do or say differently? How could you shift your thinking to recognize that the problem is a "normal" part of life? Were there other factors that made it more difficult to think flexibly, such as lack of sleep, poor diet, or little or no exercise? What could you imagine the outcome to be in this new scenario? How satisfied do you think you would be with the resolution to the problem after you approached it with flexibility?

_____

_____

_____

_____

_____

ThinkVirtues®

FOCUS 3

Visualizing and Meditating on Flexibility

How will you invite and deeply embrace the essence of Flexibility?

_____

_____

_____

_____

How do you feel after you have succeeded?

_____

_____

_____

_____

ThinkVirtues®

Flexibility

FOCUS 4

Here are some books you will enjoy reading!
They show flexibility in the characters.
You can get these books from your local library or bookstore.

If you are 4 to 8 years old, you will enjoy reading:
The Odd Egg by Emily Gravett

How is the duck flexible compared to the other birds?
What would you do in such a situation?

If you are 4 to 10 years old, you will enjoy reading:
Pumpkin Soup by Helen Cooper

Do the animals show flexibility when preparing the pumpkin soup?
Have you ever found yourself in a position
when you did not want to be flexible?

ThinkVirtues®

FOCUS 4

Thoughts become words. Words become action. Actions become character. Character becomes destiny.
©2024 ThinkVirtues, LLC. All Rights Reserved.

Flexibility

FOCUS 5

Let's be creative!

As a family, come up with a list of everyday occurrences that would typically be negatively perceived. Each person's list would include situations on it that are typical for them. Items on the list could include getting stuck in traffic, forgetting homework or a work project, being late for an important meeting or class, losing a special memento or treasured item, or breaking or damaging something that belongs to someone else.

Now look at each person's list in turn. Think of three reasons why each entry on the list might have happened. Remember: you want the person to own up to their responsibility without focusing on the negative! For example, you were late for class because you didn't allow enough time in traffic, or you overslept (or "underslept" by going to bed too late the night before), or you spent time watching television as you were getting ready for the day.

Have each family member look at their list again. What positive thing might come out of that same situation? How can you change your outlook on that event so that you can see the positive side and not just the negative? This is a valuable learning opportunity when thinking flexibly allows you to look at the situation differently and not have the same circumstance happen again.

ThinkVirtues®

FOCUS 5

Let's be creative!

Make a piece of art showing you practicing flexibility

- **Write a story or drama**
- **Write a song or poetry**
- **Create a dance**
- **Make painting or drawing**
- **Create a collage**

You can use the space below or grab some fun materials.

ThinkVirtues®

Flexibility

FOCUS 6

Family Activity

Think of a family circumstance that has been troubling for you and/or other family members. Chances are, you have developed standard patterns of behavior in dealing with this situation. As a family, create a chart that has three columns. Label the top of the first column "pros." This is where you will write down all of the possible positive aspects of this situation. It may be difficult to come up with this list, so focus on trying to see the problem through a different lens. Give yourselves plenty of time to come up with your list.

Label the second column "cons." This is probably a bit easier; if it has been a troubling family situation, you are probably very aware of the "cons" or negative aspects of this problem.

Label the third column "new ideas." Here is a great opportunity for brainstorming – trying to come up with as many different ideas and suggestions without "putting down" any that anyone suggests. Don't fully evaluate any of them yet; instead, write down as many reasonable ideas as possible. (Reasonable in this context means that you include ideas that aren't so extreme as to be silly, such as buying a mansion or winning a million dollars. Both might be nice, but they are so unlikely to happen that they become ridiculous as serious suggestions.)

Now, on a separate piece of paper, write up a family "plan." Take the reasonable and doable ideas and ask all members of the family to commit to using those ideas rather than the old, negative behaviors and habits. To make the commitments more tangible, have each family member sign their name on the bottom of the plan.

ThinkVirtues®

FOCUS 6

Family Activity

As you go through the next days and weeks, refer back to your family plan any time that formerly negative circumstance crops up. Check yourselves to be sure that everyone is honoring their commitment to follow the new plan. Together you are learning how to be more flexible in problem-solving as a family!

How do you feel about developing a family plan?

_____

_____

_____

_____

_____

_____

_____

ThinkVirtues®

Flexibility

FOCUS 7

Thinking back on the past week, focus on the time or times when you or family members were more flexible. Pat yourselves on the back for practicing such an important life skill! Think of ways you can celebrate – even with simple things such a going out for ice cream or another special treat, going for a bike ride or walk (or outside in the winter to build a snowman) as a family, playing a family game, or watching a favorite television show or movie together. The activity itself isn't what is important. Rather, it is focusing on the positive in what could otherwise have been a negative situation. Your celebration is another way of practicing flexibility!

_____

_____

_____

_____

_____

_____

ThinkVirtues®

Flexibility

REFLECTION

How flexible are you?
Take your time and write down all the ways you can become more flexible.
How does this make you feel? Good? Free?

_____

_____

_____

_____

_____

_____

_____

_____

ThinkVirtues®

REFLECTION

ThinkVirtues®

Flexibility

REFLECTION

Flexibility

REFLECTION

ThinkVirtues®

REFLECTION

ThinkVirtues®

Forgiveness

FOCUS 1

The Meaning of Forgiveness

Forgiveness means to let go of the hurt that others cause you by mistreating or taking advantage of you. We human beings are imperfect and thus make mistakes. Understanding this fact can help with the process of forgiving.

Sometimes, in order to forgive, you may have to detach yourself from the situation. Then, when you are eventually able to forgive, you will feel better.

Holding on to feelings of sadness and anger will hurt you most of all. The sooner you can forgive, the better it will be for you and everyone around you. And when you are the party in need of forgiveness? Asking for forgiveness when you have wronged another is also an important thing to practice. You will feel better when you have admitted that you made a mistake. Acknowledging that you are not perfect and have made mistakes is an important component in becoming a person of good character.

Forgiveness is not the same as condoning, forgetting, or excusing negative behavior; rather, it is a shift in attitude and release of the negative feelings within you. True forgiveness means letting go: no more indulging in self-pity or the desire to seek revenge against the person or thing that caused you harm in the first place.

You practice forgiveness by letting go of any negative feelings toward the person or thing that caused you harm. You should also forgive yourself for your shortcomings or imperfections. All human beings make mistakes, and you are no exception to this rule; therefore, you should be forgiving of your own negative actions that may have harmed those you love. Forgiving is a healthy practice for your mind and soul.

ThinkVirtues®

Forgiveness

FOCUS 1

What are three ways you can practice Forgiveness?

1. _____

2. _____

3. _____

ThinkVirtues®

Forgiveness

FOCUS 2

The Importance of Forgiveness

It is equally important to both forgive and earn forgiveness. If you don't practice forgiveness, then you are holding onto feelings of resentment which can cause you physical and emotional harm.

Resentment can lead to the desire to seek revenge; this can be destructive to you as well as everyone and everything around you. When you seek revenge, someone almost always gets hurt. The negative behavior is perpetuated and continues to grow and cause further harm.

It is of utmost importance to make forgiveness a part of your existence because it brings you and those around you peace and happiness. Similarly, seeking forgiveness allows a relationship to become peaceful and harmonious as opposed to allowing a negative behavior to destroy a relationship.

Why is it important to practice Forgiveness?

_____

_____

_____

_____

ThinkVirtues®

Forgiveness

FOCUS 2

The Importance of Forgiveness

ThinkVirtues®

Forgiveness

FOCUS 3

Visualizing and Meditating on Forgiveness

Close your eyes and think of a time when you reacted to a difficult or new situation. Close your eyes and think of a person or something that upset you in the last week. Was it a friend? What did they do? What happened? How did it make you feel? Reconcile your feelings and give them a descriptive word for the situation. What color do you see?

Imagine releasing those negative thoughts and replacing them with positive ones. Might you instead be grateful that you have had good times with your friend in the past? Though it may help, understanding the wrongdoer's motives and intentions is not as important as forgiving them for their shortcomings.

Imagine how peaceful and happy you will feel by not holding a grudge or feeling resentful. Give that peaceful and happy feeling a name and a color. Try to remember this whenever someone does you wrong.

_____

_____

_____

_____

ThinkVirtues®

FOCUS 3

Visualizing and Meditating on Forgiveness

How will you invite and deeply embrace the essence of Forgiveness?

_____

_____

_____

_____

How do you feel after you have succeeded?

_____

_____

_____

_____

_____

VIRTUES IN ACTION - Empowering Kids and Families to Connect, Grow, and Thrive

ThinkVirtues®

Forgiveness

FOCUS 4

Here are some books you will enjoy reading!
They show forgiveness in the characters.
You can get these books from your local library or bookstore.

If you are 4 to 9 years old, you will enjoy reading:
The Forgiveness Garden by Lauren Thompson

Why does the girl choose to forgive in order to move past the situation?
How can hatred and revenge be overcome by forgiveness?
Is it easy to forgive? Think of a time when you had to forgive someone.
How did you feel?

If you are 5 to 10 years old, you will enjoy reading:
The Grudge Keeper by Mara Rockliff

Why do the townspeople take their grudges to Cornelius the Grudge Keeper? Why do grudges hold us back from achieving things?

If you are 9 to 12 years old, you will enjoy reading:
The Lemonade Crime by Jacqueline Davies
Sequel to **The Lemonade War**

How is forgiveness determined by law?
Is the trial just? What morals do we learn from this book?

Thoughts become words. Words become action. Actions become character. Character becomes destiny.
©2024 ThinkVirtues, LLC. All Rights Reserved.

ThinkVirtues®

Forgiveness

FOCUS 4

ThinkVirtues®

Forgiveness

FOCUS 5

Let's be creative!

As a family, come up with a list of everyday occurrences that would typically cause hurt and need forgiveness. Write a letter to someone (or something) who has done you wrong, whether or not you have forgiven them in the past. Use this exercise to forgive that person (or thing) if you haven't done so already.

In this letter express your hurt and your plan to forgive them for the hurt they caused you. Express in writing each step that you took in order to be able to forgive them.

After going through that process, express how you feel about the situation as well as that person. Consider and ultimately decide whether or not to actually send the letter to the person. (If you have already forgiven them and the matter is in the past, you may want to use this letter as an exercise only. If, on the other hand, you had not yet forgiven them, you may want to send the letter.)

Be sure to keep this letter (or a copy) for your journal.

ThinkVirtues®

Forgiveness

FOCUS 5

Let's be creative!

Make a piece of art showing you practicing forgiveness

- **Write a story or drama**
- **Write a song or poetry**
- **Create a dance**
- **Make painting or drawing**
- **Create a collage**

You can use the space below or grab some fun materials.

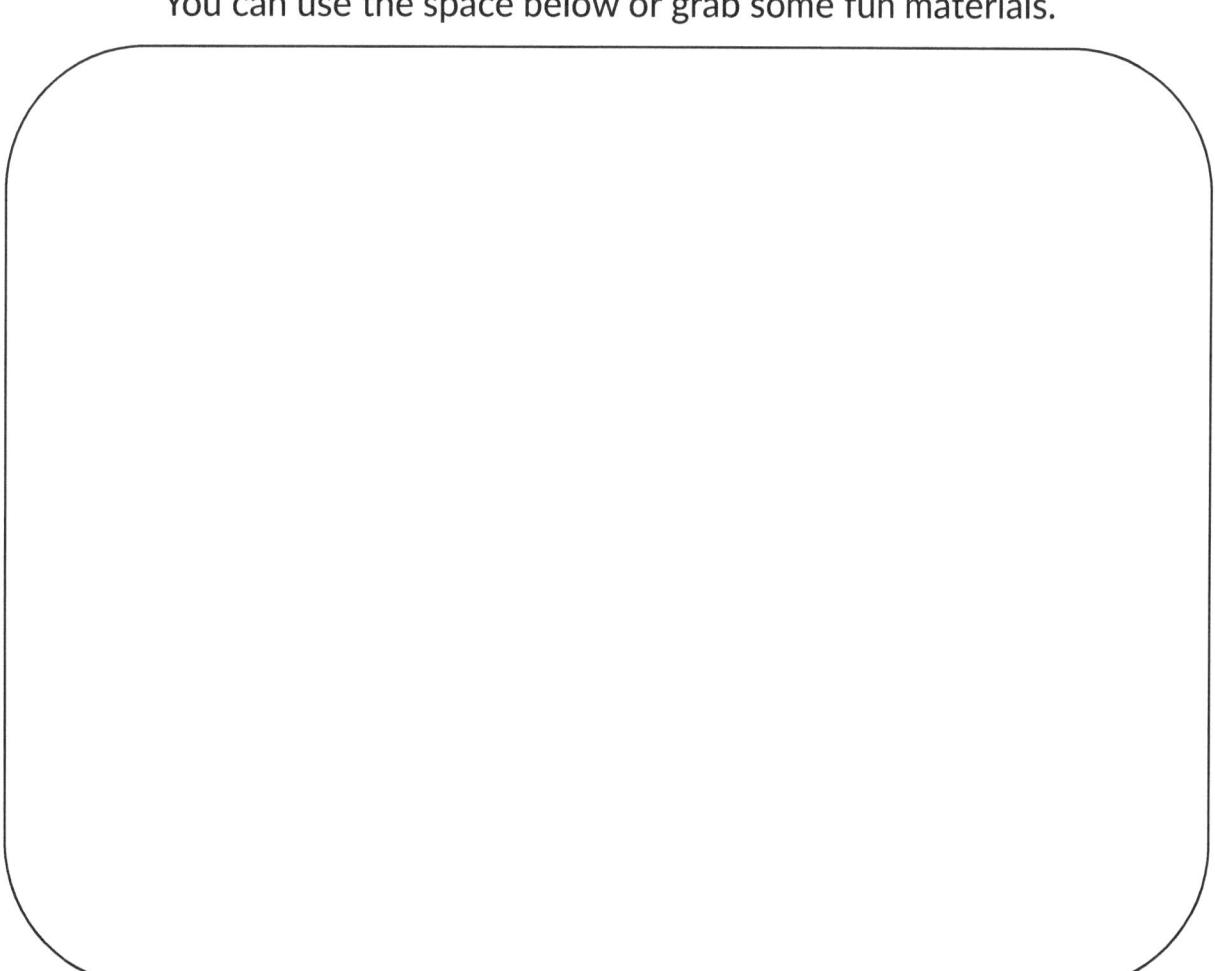

ThinkVirtues®

Forgiveness

FOCUS 6

Family Activity

Use this as an opportunity to have a family forum during which each family member thinks of a family situation that was hurtful. Take turns expressing your hurt to each other. Immediately after, point out all of the good things each person has done for you in the past. Point out all of their good points and positive character and personality traits. Focus on the love that you have for them. Acknowledge their love for you.

As you go through this process, you will notice that you have softened and are no longer as angry or hurt because you can see the bigger picture and were able to step outside of the one incident that caused you pain. You are able to forgive.

Let your family member know that you forgive them. Then pass the baton to the next family member to express their hurt. While you are going through this process, be sure to practice forgiveness toward one another and practice tact in your expressions. Be sure to give each person the time they need to get everything off of their chest. You may need to revisit this family activity; you may need extra time to complete it. Be patient, and give love to one another as you each go through this taxing, difficult, and painful process.

ThinkVirtues®

Forgiveness

FOCUS 6

Family Activity

How do you feel about this family activity?

_____

_____

_____

_____

_____

_____

_____

_____

_____

ThinkVirtues®

Forgiveness

FOCUS 7

Use this day to reflect on the week's activities. How many people did you forgive? How do you feel about them? How do you feel about yourself for being able to forgive the person or people who harmed you?

In releasing these negative energies and feelings and replacing them with positive ones, do you feel lighter, healthier, and happier? Notice the good feelings that have replaced the negative ones.

_____

_____

_____

_____

_____

_____

_____

ThinkVirtues®

Forgiveness
REFLECTION

Who do you forgive? How do you forgive? Why do you forgive? Forgiveness is a heart centered virtue, the more we can practice it, the happier we feel.

Sometimes we need to forgive ourselves for some of the things we wish we had done better. How do you practice forgiveness best?

_____

_____

_____

_____

_____

_____

_____

ThinkVirtues®

Forgiveness

REFLECTION

ThinkVirtues®

Forgiveness
REFLECTION

Forgiveness
REFLECTION

ThinkVirtues®

Forgiveness
REFLECTION

Thoughts become words. Words become action. Actions become character. Character becomes destiny.

ThinkVirtues®

ThinkVirtues®

Thoughts become words. Words become action. Actions become character. Character becomes destiny.
©2024 ThinkVirtues, LLC. All Rights Reserved.

ThinkVirtues®

Generosity

FOCUS 1

The Meaning of Generosity

Generosity is sharing things, talents, or time with other people with no expectation of getting anything in return. A generous person is happy to share time, money, possessions, or food and does not begrudge giving to others.

Generosity is not based on a person's economic status or financial situation. Even poor people can be generous. Generosity comes from the heart and is based on good intentions to consider giving or doing good for someone else or society as a whole. Generosity, then, is a focus on others rather than self.

We practice generosity when we seek ways to donate our time, talent, or things. Often a tragedy or natural disaster prompts us to be more generous. When the news is filled with images of a disaster such as a hurricane, tornado, flood, or fire, we want to give to help alleviate the suffering that results.

While giving generously in times of great disaster and need is commendable, the virtue of generosity is one that can and should be practiced in everyday, ordinary life. Sharing with siblings, letting a friend go first, taking turns, listening carefully to another person, giving credit to someone else's ideas or work, doing an unexpected act of kindness, or sitting quietly with someone can all be acts of generosity.

It is easier to be generous when a person has a sense of gratitude for what he has. The "Theory of Plenty" is an underlying belief that there are sufficient resources for a person's needs to be satisfied. Believing in such a theory makes it easier to recognize that generosity will not create scarcity for the giver. Being grateful for what we have makes us more willing to share our plenty with others.

ThinkVirtues®

FOCUS 1

What are three ways you can practice Generosity?

1. _____

2. _____

3. _____

Generosity

FOCUS 2

The Importance of Generosity

Generosity obviously helps those people who need it. It is easy to see that generosity helps make the world a better place, especially for those whose life circumstances – either temporary (from a disaster, for example) or permanent (in developing nations plagued by drought, for example) – can be drastically improved when others are generous.

What has consistently been shown to be true is that generous people are happier people. Generosity opens up the heart and expands a person's thinking to focus more on others. Focusing on others rather than only on ourselves makes us better people. Generosity is rooted in selflessness. Although indirectly, there is a benefit to the one who is generous. In fact, generosity may be a key to leading a healthy and happy life.

Being generous often inspires others to be generous. It isn't just that we feel better about ourselves when we are generous, but we also have a greater sense of connection to others. This is especially true when our own generosity is expanded through the generosity triggered in someone else.

Why is it important to practice Generosity?

_____

_____

_____

ThinkVirtues®

Generosity

FOCUS 2

The Importance of Generosity

Generosity

FOCUS 3

Visualizing and Meditating on Generosity

There is an ancient story told that illustrates generosity. Share this story with your family. As you read it with them, have them close their eyes to visualize the players in this story – from the poor woman to the rich people. Once the story has been read aloud, everyone should remain quiet and still for a few moments to mentally review the images in his mind's eye. Discuss the meaning of the story and how it illustrates generosity?

She was an elderly widow who was very poor. She wanted to give generously, but what she was able to give seemed so pitiful compared with the rich villagers who were standing nearby.

It took her quite awhile to move through the crowds that were near the donation center. Her aching bones made her footsteps slow, and her sense of being out of place made her cautious. What would they think of her? Would her little gift even make a difference?

She shrugged her shoulders as if to shake off her own doubt and uncertainty. With her eyes focused on the donation box, she continued forcing her feet forward. Although her body was old, tired, and stooped, her eyes glistened in anticipation of being able to help, of offering what she could to those in need.

Finally, she arrived at the donation box. Digging deep into her pockets, she pulled out the last two coins she owned. They were all she had – but they represented only a few cents – a paltry amount. She dropped the change into the slot and smiled as she heard them clink on the bottom.

ThinkVirtues®

Generosity

FOCUS 3

Visualizing and Meditating on Generosity

As she turned to make her way slowly home, she realized that she was humming and that her steps seemed easier, lighter somehow despite the aching in her bones.

There were rich people standing in the crowds. They, too, had given to the donation box. Unlike the old widow, they wanted to be sure that others saw what they gave – paper money that, while large in amount, represented only a very small portion of their huge fortunes. Still, they thought, theirs were the donations that would make the greatest difference to the needy people for whom the donation box was meant.

So they laughed when they heard the old widow's coins drop into the box. "Her measly coins won't make any difference," said one person. "And her gift is nothing compared with what I gave," exclaimed another. They continued to mock the widow and congratulate themselves for how much they had given, especially in comparison with the widow's gift.

But the old widow had actually given MORE. She gave all that she had – her last two coins. The rich people's gifts were much larger in actual money, but they gave only a little bit from their large fortunes.

Questions for family discussion:
Who was more generous, the old widow or the rich people?
What does this story teach us about generosity?
What does it mean for us as a family when it comes to generosity?

VIRTUES IN ACTION - Empowering Kids and Families to Connect, Grow, and Thrive

ThinkVirtues®

Generosity

FOCUS 3

Visualizing and Meditating on Generosity

How will you invite and deeply embrace the essence of Generosity?

_____

_____

_____

_____

_____

_____

_____

_____

Thoughts become words. Words become action. Actions become character. Character becomes destiny.

ThinkVirtues®

Generosity

FOCUS 3

Visualizing and Meditating on Generosity

How do you feel after you have succeeded?

___

___

___

___

___

___

___

___

VIRTUES IN ACTION - Empowering Kids and Families to Connect, Grow, and Thrive

ThinkVirtues®

Generosity

FOCUS 4

Here are some books you will enjoy reading!
They show generosity in the characters.
You can get these books from your local library or bookstore.

If you are 4 to 9 years old, you will enjoy reading:
The Quiltmaker's Gift by Jeff Brumbeau

How do the king's feelings change as he continues to be giving?
What do we gain when we give to others?

If you are 5 to 10 years old, you will enjoy reading:
Listen to the Wind by Greg Mortensen

How do the villagers show generosity to the stranger?
What is achieved through generosity?

If you are 8 to 10 years old, you will enjoy reading:
The Can Man by Laura E. Williams & Craig Orback

How does the Can Man impact Tim's generosity?
How does generosity help make Tim aware of social concerns
in the neighborhood?

Thoughts become words. Words become action. Actions become character. Character becomes destiny.
©2024 ThinkVirtues, LLC. All Rights Reserved.

ThinkVirtues®

FOCUS 4

Thoughts become words. Words become action. Actions become character. Character becomes destiny.

Generosity

FOCUS 5

Let's be creative!

Create something to depict the story of the woman and the two coins. Include the response of the rich bystanders who looked down at her. Also include what you think your response would be if you had been there to witness the event. Share with the other members of your family what your artistic representation – whether words, music, movement, or visual arts - means to you as the artist.

_____

_____

_____

_____

_____

_____

_____

ThinkVirtues®

FOCUS 5

Let's be creative!

Make a piece of art showing you practicing generosity.

- **Write a story or drama**
- **Write a song or poetry**
- **Create a dance**
- **Make painting or drawing**
- **Create a collage**

You can use the space below or grab some fun materials.

Generosity

FOCUS 6

Family Activity

As a family, find a person or cause that especially touches your hearts. Think about how you could be generous with that person, people, or cause you selected. Remember that generosity can be of time, talents, or things. Can you think of ways to be generous in all three areas?

As you decide on ways to be generous, consider your own heart. Are you giving out of generosity, or would you begrudge what you give? Giving from the heart is at the center of generosity. Remember the old widow. Hers was a gift from the heart; for the rich people, their gifts came from vanity, to impress others over how much they could give.

ThinkVirtues®

Generosity

FOCUS 6

Family Activity

How do you feel about this family activity?

ThinkVirtues®

FOCUS 7

Generosity is much more than just giving. Generosity is more a gift of the heart than of the wallet. Consider all the examples of generosity you have seen this week. Did your child want to share their toys with "poor people?"

Or perhaps another wanted to give their whole allowance to a worthy person or cause. Think of those who are generous with their time – who spend seemingly endless hours visiting the sick, listening to those whose voices aren't always heard, or working on behalf of those in need. What about people who use their talents as volunteers so that others' lives are easier or happier?

When you are generous, how do you feel? How can you keep a spirit of generosity in your heart and home? What people or projects are you willing to commit to with your time, talents, or things? Are you able to be generous, even if your gift(s) are anonymous?

Write how it feels when you are generous. How does it feel when you have chosen not to be generous? How can you make your actions reflect the virtue of generosity?

_____

_____

_____

_____

ThinkVirtues®

Generosity
FOCUS 7

ThinkVirtues®

Generosity

REFLECTION

How does generosity from others make you feel? How do you feel when you are being generous to others? Write all about it here in these pages, about everything that shows up for you, and about how generosity shows up in your world.

ThinkVirtues®

Generosity

REFLECTION

Thoughts become words. Words become action. Actions become character. Character becomes destiny.
©2024 ThinkVirtues, LLC. All Rights Reserved.

ThinkVirtues®

Generosity

REFLECTION

___

___

___

___

___

___

___

___

___

Thoughts become words. Words become action. Actions become character. Character becomes destiny.
©2024 ThinkVirtues, LLC. All Rights Reserved.

ThinkVirtues®

Generosity
REFLECTION

ThinkVirtues®

REFLECTION

ThinkVirtues®

Generosity
REFLECTION

Thoughts become words. Words become action. Actions become character. Character becomes destiny.
©2024 ThinkVirtues, LLC. All Rights Reserved.

ThinkVirtues®

Thoughts become words. Words become action. Actions become character. Character becomes destiny.
©2024 ThinkVirtues, LLC. All Rights Reserved.

ThinkVirtues®

Joyfulness

FOCUS 1

The Meaning of Joyfulness

Joyfulness is a feeling or emotion of positivity that you experience or help to cause in another person; it is something you show and express when alone and around other people. Joyfulness means a deep happiness, peacefulness, and enthusiasm for life. It includes a positive attitude, and joyful people are people who smile readily and often.

Joyfulness is a state of graceful happiness, of optimism. When faced with a difficult situation, a joyful person handles it as if he can see beyond the current circumstances and still recognize the happiness in life. Circumstances change, but underlying joy is constant, and a joyful person is filled with hope and faith that things are going to be better.

Joyful people tend to handle difficult situations better than negative people who are likely to spoil the mood of those around them. Joyful people are attractive to others, and they are fun to be around. While there are times when joyfulness seems to bubble up on its own, it is also a deliberate choice to be joyful.

Practicing joyfulness means putting on a smile and seeking ways to be happy or grateful whenever possible. The more you smile, the happier you feel inside. Furthermore, it spreads a feeling of joy to those around you, and it often becomes reciprocal. Spreading joy with a smile, a kind word, or a spirit of gratitude brings joy to others – and then it returns, multiplied, to you.

ThinkVirtues®

Joyfulness

FOCUS 1

What are three ways you can practice Joyfulness?

1. _____

2. _____

3. _____

Joyfulness

FOCUS 2

The Importance of Joyfulness

It is more fun to be around joyful people than negative people. Being around someone who exhibits joy lightens everyone's day and mood and encourages others to also be joyful.

Joyfulness also requires sensitivity to another's pain – whether physical or emotional. The circumstances themselves do not inspire joy; rather, they inspire an internal sense of well-being that allows for the deeper feelings of joy to eventually shine through despite negative situations or circumstances. Joyfulness is best expressed and shared when another person is simply "down in the dumps" or grumpy rather than when she is going through a devastating life experience (i.e. death or serious illness).

Joyfulness shifts the focus to positive things instead of negative. Joyful people look for the good in others or in difficult situations as they celebrate goodness and beauty. Joyfulness inspires us to take on the tasks at hand as we inspire others to do the same.

Although it is difficult to be joyful in painful circumstances, joyfulness can be a beacon of light and hope on a dark day. Like all other virtues, joyfulness is contagious. One person's joy spreads readily to others. It is then that joyfulness touches everyone in a special way and enriches and brightens life for others as well as for the joyful person.

ThinkVirtues®

Joyfulness
FOCUS 2

The Importance of Joyfulness

Why is it important to practice Joyfulness?

_____

_____

_____

_____

_____

_____

_____

_____

ThinkVirtues®

FOCUS 3

Visualizing and Meditating on Joyfulness

Think of a time when you were joyful. How did you feel? What was the response of others when you were joyful? Imagine looking in the mirror. How would others have known you were joyful? What kind of expression showed on your face? What other actions did you note?

Now think of a time when you were sad or discouraged. Was there anyone in your life who brought joyfulness to you? What kind of expression showed on their face? What actions made you think they were joyful?

Now imagine seeing someone who sad or who is negative. How can you respond with joyfulness? What will you do and say to express joyfulness? What will you do to demonstrate sensitivity to the other person's pain?

How will you invite and deeply embrace the essence of Joyfulness?

_____

_____

_____

_____

ThinkVirtues®

Joyfulness

FOCUS 3

Visualizing and Meditating on Joyfulness

How do you feel after you have succeeded?

ThinkVirtues®

Joyfulness

FOCUS 4

Here are some books you will enjoy reading!
They show joyfulness in the characters.
You can get these books from your local library or bookstore.

If you are 3 to 6 years old, you will enjoy reading:
Cheer Up Your Teddy Bear, Emily Brown! by Cressida Cowell

*Do you think Emily does the right thing by trying
to bring joy to the teddy bear?
What could she have done differently to make the teddy bear joyful?
How do you find joy in life?*

If you are 5 to 9 years old, you will enjoy reading:
Something Beautiful by Sharon Dennis Wyeth

*How does the little girl seek joy in her adventures?
How can we find joyfulness through beauty in everyday things?*

ThinkVirtues®

Joyfulness

FOCUS 4

Thoughts become words. Words become action. Actions become character. Character becomes destiny.

ThinkVirtues®

Joyfulness

FOCUS 5

Let's be creative!

Use your favorite means of creative expression (words, music, movement, or visual arts) to create something that represents joy. Draw a picture of a home filled with joy. Write a poem or song that brings out joy in you. Does a walk on the beach or in the park bring you joy? Is there a person who brings you joy?

What brings joy to you? Your artistic representation can be realistic or abstract and should reflect light and happiness. Let your creativity freely flow as that experience will also likely bring a sense of joyfulness to you.

_____

_____

_____

_____

_____

_____

ThinkVirtues®

Joyfulness

FOCUS 5

Let's be creative!

Make a piece of art showing you practicing joyfulness.

- **Write a story or drama**
- **Write a song or poetry**
- **Create a dance**
- **Make painting or drawing**
- **Create a collage**

You can use the space below or grab some fun materials.

Thoughts become words. Words become action. Actions become character. Character becomes destiny.
©2024 ThinkVirtues, LLC. All Rights Reserved.

ThinkVirtues®

Joyfulness
FOCUS 6

Family Activity

As a family, either at a family meeting or around the dinner table, talk about joyfulness, how it feels, and what it looks like. Ask each family member to share a time when they felt joy. Describe what you visualized on Focus 3: how did it feel, how did others respond, and what did it look like? Make a point of smiling as you share your story!

If you have experienced joy, a smile is a natural outward expression of that. Think of at least three times when you can practice joy with a smile in a situation or place where you perhaps have not been joyful. Tell your family about those times, and what you will do to bring joy to that situation. Use language such as, "I felt joyful when_____," and, "I am going to bring joyfulness by _____."

You could also find joy in a shared family activity. Watch a joyful, uplifting movie such as Disney's Frozen. Make up other, silly lyrics to one of the songs from the movie, or try to act out one of the silly parts in the movie.

Play a fun game together like "Twister." Laughing together as a family brings a sense of joy. Enjoy each other while doing something that is just for fun. Talk about the joyful feelings you created by engaging together in fun family activities – whatever you choose!

ThinkVirtues®

Joyfulness

FOCUS 6

Family Activity

How do you feel about this family activity?

_____

_____

_____

_____

_____

_____

_____

_____

ThinkVirtues®

Joyfulness

FOCUS 7

Just thinking about joyfulness will probably make you feel more joy! Make a commitment to smile at everyone you see in a day – whether a family member, friend, or stranger. Focus your thoughts on the positive, perhaps using gratitude as a way to turn your negative thoughts into positive ones.

Who is the most negative person you know? How can you bring joy to that person? It may be as simple as offering a warm smile each time you see them. Make a commitment to share joy with that person, and keep a record of your experiences with them in a journal or diary.

_____

_____

_____

_____

_____

_____

ThinkVirtues®

Joyfulness

FOCUS 7

ThinkVirtues®

Joyfulness
REFLECTION

How does being joyful make you feel inside? Write all about it here. Write down all the ways you practice joyfulness.

_____

_____

_____

_____

_____

_____

_____

_____

_____

ThinkVirtues®

Joyfulness
REFLECTION

Joyfulness
REFLECTION

ThinkVirtues®

Joyfulness
REFLECTION

_____

_____

_____

_____

_____

_____

_____

_____

_____

ThinkVirtues®

Joyfulness
REFLECTION

ThinkVirtues®

REFLECTION

ThinkVirtues®

Thoughts become words. Words become action. Actions become character. Character becomes destiny.
©2024 ThinkVirtues, LLC. All Rights Reserved.

ThinkVirtues®

Love

FOCUS 1

The Meaning of Love

Love is at the core of all virtues and has been expressed as being the greatest. Love has many meanings and interpretations ranging from personal affection, like loving your mother, to romantic love, to loving a thing. However, as a virtue, love is portrayed in displaying kindness, affection, compassion, and patience for another being. When you love someone, you are unselfish, benevolently concerned, and loyal to them.

You take care of those you love, even if it means sacrificing something for yourself. Love shows up everywhere around you in books, art, movies, poetry, songs – just about everywhere you look. Because love is a powerful emotion and virtue, it moves you in a deep and meaningful way. It is the basis of most interpersonal relationships.

You practice love by showing kindness, caring, and compassion toward others. You also show patience in their shortcomings or life's journey. You take care of your family, friends, and pets. You may show your love by giving hugs and kisses – or by a simple, kind word. Showing respect and understanding to those you love is another way of showing them you love them. You are also considerate of their feelings, desires, and goals; and you show your support when they need you. For example, if you like to show love through kisses and hugs, you show your true love and consideration by respecting another person's sense of personal space – and ask for permission to hug or kiss him.

You must remember to love yourself first and foremost. Without love for yourself, it is difficult to love another. Love fills you up to overflowing.

ThinkVirtues®

Love

FOCUS 1

What are three ways you can practice Love?

1. _____

2. _____

3. _____

Thoughts become words. Words become action. Actions become character. Character becomes destiny.
©2024 ThinkVirtues, LLC. All Rights Reserved.

ThinkVirtues®

Love

FOCUS 2

The Importance of Love

Love gives your life deeper meaning. Both loving someone and being loved makes you happy and fills you with faith, hope, and joy. It gives you a deeper sense of purpose. When you love someone, you are compelled to take care of them, to be there for them. Love brings out the best in you and everyone around you.

Love brings your family closer together and creates an unbreakable and long-lasting bond. Love even has a significant, positive impact on your physical health and wellbeing.

Dr. Dean Ornish makes a powerful statement about love when he says, "I am not aware of any other factor in medicine – not diet, not smoking, not exercise, not stress, not genetics, not drugs, not surgery – that has a greater impact on our quality of life, incidence of illness, and premature death from all causes. Love and intimacy are at the root of what makes us sick and what makes us well, what causes sadness and what brings happiness, what makes us suffer, and what leads to healing."

Despite the circumstances, it is the love for and of your support system and/or your family and friends that makes everything okay in the end.

ThinkVirtues®

Love

FOCUS 2

The Importance of Love

Why is it important to practice Love?

_____

_____

_____

_____

_____

_____

_____

_____

FOCUS 3

Visualizing and Meditating on Love

Close your eyes and give yourself a moment to think of someone you love. Think of all of the reasons you love that person. Think of all of the reasons they love you. Imagine yourself being generous, caring, and kind to them and receiving the same in return. Know that all will be beautiful and okay for you and your loved ones.

How does this make you feel? Give this feeling a color and a place.

_____

_____

_____

_____

_____

_____

ThinkVirtues®

Love

FOCUS 3

Visualizing and Meditating on Love

How do you feel after you have succeeded?

_____

_____

_____

_____

_____

_____

_____

ThinkVirtues®

Love

FOCUS 3

Visualizing and Meditating on Love

As a family, start calling attention to the differences between "like" and "love." What are the things you like about people? What behaviors make them likeable?

What are the things you don't like about some people? What behaviors make them seem unlikeable?

Have each person think of a person they don't like. Be careful about not using this as an excuse to talk about someone who isn't "liked"!

Now think about learning to love that person – as he or she is – with no expectation for anything in return from that person.

What one thing could you do to demonstrate love for that person?

Practice doing that one thing every day for a week.

After one week, how do you feel about that person now?

Now add another action to demonstrate love for that person.

As you are more comfortable about acting out of love, think of another person you could love whom you don't like. Or think of more ways to continue growing in love for the person you selected.

_____

_____

_____

_____

ThinkVirtues®

Love

FOCUS 3

Visualizing and Meditating on Love

ThinkVirtues®

Love

FOCUS 4

Here are some books you will enjoy reading!
They show love in the characters.
You can get these books from your local library or bookstore.

If you are 3 to 9 years old, you will enjoy reading:
Love You Forever by Robert Munsch

*How does the love of the mother transfer to the child?
How does the love change as time passes on?*

If you are 7 to 10 years old, you will enjoy reading:
The Miraculous Journey of Edward Tulane by Kate DiCamillo

*How does a fragile, breakable heart learn to love and lose in this story?
In which ways is love a reoccurring theme in
Edward Tulane's path to redemption?*

ThinkVirtues®

Love

FOCUS 4

ThinkVirtues®

Love

FOCUS 5

Let's be creative!

Make 10 fortune cookies! For this virtue create fortune cookie notes that express your love for other beings. Have each family member make 10 notes. Save these sayings for the family activity.

1. _____

2. _____

3. _____

4. _____

5. _____

6. _____

7. _____

8. _____

9. _____

10. _____

ThinkVirtues®

Love

FOCUS 5

Let's be creative!

Make a piece of art showing you practicing love.

- **Write a story or drama**
- **Write a song or poetry**
- **Create a dance**
- **Make painting or drawing**
- **Create a collage**

You can use the space below or grab some fun materials.

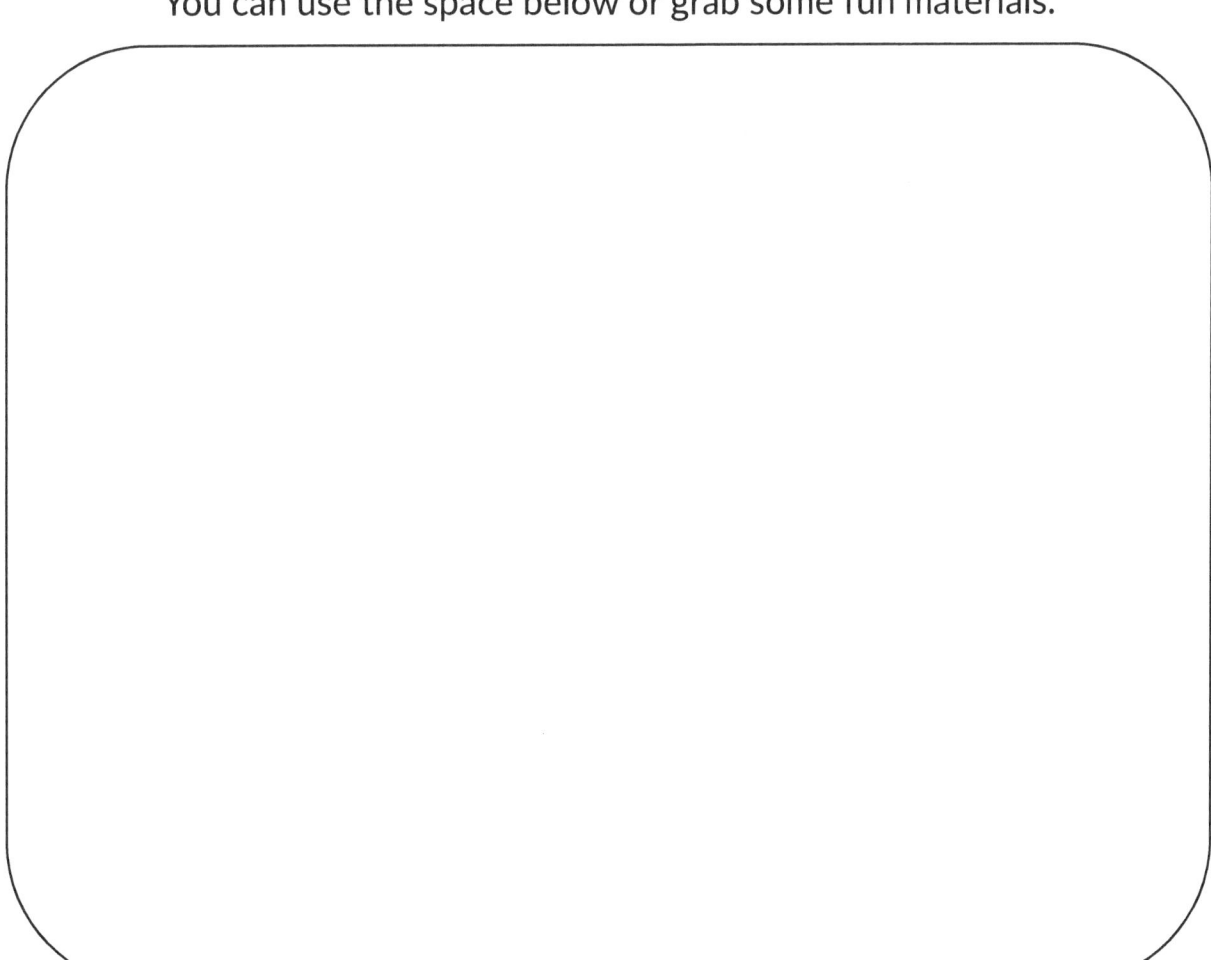

Love

FOCUS 6

Family Activity

Make a Love Jar!

Think of special ways to show one another that you love each other. We suggest the following ways that you can show your love for another, but feel free to do your own thing.

1) Express your gratitude for one another. Thank your parents.
2) Send a love note/card. (You can make this yourself. It will mean more!)
3) Give flowers (or pick flowers from your backyard).
4) Buy or create a special gift.
5) Keep negative criticism to a minimum. Remember, your point of view is not the only point of view. That goes for everyone!
6) Offer your kindness to one another.
7) Make time for one another.
8) Be thoroughly generous with your time and affection with one another.
9) Be forgiving.

ThinkVirtues®

Love

FOCUS 6

Family Activity

How do you feel about this family activity?

ThinkVirtues®

Love

FOCUS 7

Take this time to share and acknowledge one another for all of the wonderful things you did for each other. This is a great time to pull out your fortune cookie sayings and share them with your loved ones! Enjoy each other's love and companionship. Life is nothing if not for our loved ones around us. And, of course, don't forget: hugs and kisses for everyone! And not the chocolate kind.

_____

_____

_____

_____

_____

_____

_____

ThinkVirtues®

Love

FOCUS 7

Love

REFLECTION

You were born worthy of love and belonging. Love always begins with self-love. Love yourself because you are precious expression of life. You have a special gift with in you, and loving yourself will allow you to open up and show it to the world.

ThinkVirtues®

Love

REFLECTION

VIRTUES IN ACTION - Empowering Kids and Families to Connect, Grow, and Thrive

ThinkVirtues®

Love

REFLECTION

___

Thoughts become words. Words become action. Actions become character. Character becomes destiny.
©2024 ThinkVirtues, LLC. All Rights Reserved.

ThinkVirtues®

Love

REFLECTION

_____

_____

_____

_____

_____

_____

_____

_____

_____

_____

Thoughts become words. Words become action. Actions become character. Character becomes destiny.
©2024 ThinkVirtues, LLC. All Rights Reserved.

ThinkVirtues®

Love

REFLECTION

ThinkVirtues®

Love

REFLECTION

_____

_____

_____

_____

_____

_____

_____

_____

_____

_____

ThinkVirtues®

Thoughts become words. Words become action. Actions become character. Character becomes destiny.
©2024 ThinkVirtues, LLC. All Rights Reserved.

Patience

FOCUS 1

The Meaning of Patience

According to Dr. Kourosh Dini, patience is "the skill of allowing and supporting a process to develop at its own pace." It may mean delaying something that you want in order to respect someone else's rights. For example, when you see a friend who is in conversation with someone else, showing patience means that you wait until their conversation is finished before starting your own conversation with them.

Patience also means staying calm when circumstances seem to slow you down. Sometimes, adults lose patience when dealing with a child who is having a tantrum or when dealing with an elderly person who is slower at moving and thinking. Patience means being accepting and tolerant of a situation and not responding by shouting or with unpleasant words.

Greater patience leads to better relationships with others. Impatience usually results in some level of anger toward others. By exercising patience, life is easier, calmer, and more pleasant for you and the others in your life.

Patience reminds you that you aren't always in control. It can teach you self-control and help you remember to stop and smell the roses – both literally and figuratively. Patience keeps you from making impulsive decisions and allows time for you to make considered and carefully thought-out decisions.

We practice patience when we recognize circumstances where we tend to feel impatient. Recognizing those times is a first step to shifting from impatience to patience. Sometimes it helps to breathe deeply and count slowly to ten before responding to that feeling of impatience that wells up within us.

ThinkVirtues®

FOCUS 1

The Meaning of Patience

Realize that patience is an internal response to circumstances – often those over which we have no control. When you are stuck in traffic, when there is a long line at the grocery store, or when a child is taking "too long" to do something, pay attention to your feelings. Then deliberately work to change how you respond to the situation. Remember that patience is an internal response to an external situation. In other words, it isn't caused by something outside ourselves; rather it is practiced by how we respond to those circumstances. With time, we can practice patience and get better at incorporating it into our daily lives.

What are three ways you can practice Patience?

1. _____

2. _____

3. _____

Patience

FOCUS 2

The Importance of Patience

In our fast-paced world, it is sometimes difficult to exhibit true patience. But being patient leads to calmness and a sense of inner strength. Impatience often leads to lashing out at someone else – an action that we would eventually regret. Patience, though, allows us to recognize and respect the feelings of another person, thereby contributing to greater peace and harmony in the relationship.

Looking at a situation from another perspective can help us practice patience. By doing so, we not only learn patience, but we create greater awareness of how another person might feel. Helping another person to feel better is, in the long run, more satisfying for both people in the situation. Recognizing that fact is important.

Practicing patience reduces lashing out, uttering angry words, and taking other hurtful actions that tend to make a situation more difficult. Patience has the opposite effect; it helps make things better and easier for everyone.

ThinkVirtues®

FOCUS 2

The Importance of Patience

Why is it important to practice Patience?

___

___

___

___

___

___

___

___

ThinkVirtues®

FOCUS 3

Visualizing and Meditating on Patience

Who is the most patient person you know? What behaviors do you notice when that person is practicing patience? What is the impact of their patience on the people around them?

Now imagine your own response to frustrating situations. How patient are you? What could you do that would exhibit patience? What would patience look like? How can you show more patience? What steps can you take that would help to develop patience?

_____

_____

_____

_____

_____

_____

ThinkVirtues®

FOCUS 3

Visualizing and Meditating on Patience

ThinkVirtues®

Patience

FOCUS 3

Visualizing and Meditating on Patience

How will you invite and deeply embrace the essence of Patience?

_____

_____

_____

_____

_____

_____

_____

_____

_____

ThinkVirtues®

FOCUS 3

Visualizing and Meditating on Patience

How do you feel after you have succeeded?

_____

_____

_____

_____

_____

_____

_____

_____

ThinkVirtues®

Patience

FOCUS 4

Here are some books you will enjoy reading!
They show patience in the characters.
You can get these books from your local library or bookstore.

If you are 4 to 9 years old, you will enjoy reading:
Interrupting Chicken by David Ezra Stein

How does the little red chicken ruin the bedtime stories?
Which virtue does the little chicken lack?
What can we learn from his behavior?

If you are 5 to 12 years old, you will enjoy reading:
Salt in His Shoes: Michael Jordan in Pursuit of a Dream
by Deloris Jordan

How does Michael Jordan show patience through his growing years?
Which lessons does Michael Jordan's story teach us?
Can you relate to any of the feelings young Jordan experiences?

ThinkVirtues®

Patience

FOCUS 4

___
___
___
___
___
___
___
___
___

ThinkVirtues®

Patience

FOCUS 5

Let's be creative!

Create a family skit that illustrates examples of both patience and impatience. For example, pretend you are waiting in a long line. What would you do and say to exhibit patience? How would you exhibit impatience?

Give each family member a turn to be the actor expressing both patience and impatience in different situations.

Discuss how you felt when observing the actor. How could you readily see that the person was patient/impatient? What behaviors did each display?

_____

_____

_____

_____

_____

_____

ThinkVirtues®

Patience

FOCUS 5

Let's be creative!

Make a piece of art showing you practicing patience.

- **Write a story or drama**
- **Write a song or poetry**
- **Create a dance**
- **Make painting or drawing**
- **Create a collage**

You can use the space below or grab some fun materials.

ThinkVirtues®

Patience

FOCUS 6

Family Activity

Think of at least two situations when you tend to be impatient.

What other behaviors could you choose to help practice patience in those same situations? What would it look like?

Act out examples of patience for these two situations with the rest of your family. As each person finishes their actions, talk about how it feels when you see a family member exhibiting patience.

Are there other situations in which you could practice greater patience?

Ask family members to help you recognize when you are impatient and how you could better practice patience.

_____

_____

_____

_____

ThinkVirtues®

FOCUS 6

Family Activity

How do you feel about this family activity?

_____

_____

_____

_____

_____

_____

_____

_____

Patience

FOCUS 7

There is an old "prayer" that has been often quoted when it comes to patience. "Lord, give me patience – and give it to me right now!" Sometimes, it takes patience to learn to be patient!

Think back on the family activity. When did you feel most impatient? Were there other times when family members suggested you could be more patient? How can you take steps to become more patient? Remember – it is a learning process! Be kind to yourself as you learn the virtue of patience! It will not come in an instant, but you can congratulate yourself for taking the steps you need to develop more patience with your family, friends, peers, and colleagues.

_____

_____

_____

_____

_____

_____

ThinkVirtues®

FOCUS 7

VIRTUES IN ACTION - Empowering Kids and Families to Connect, Grow, and Thrive

ThinkVirtues®

Patience

REFLECTION

How do you practice patience? How does it make you feel? Write all about it here. Do you wish people were more patient with you? Do you assert yourself in this way? Feel free to assert yourself respectfully and ask people to please be patient with you when you need extra time. Write about your experience with patience here.

_____

_____

_____

_____

_____

_____

_____

ThinkVirtues®

Patience

REFLECTION

ThinkVirtues®

REFLECTION

ThinkVirtues®

REFLECTION

___

___

___

___

___

___

___

___

___

Thoughts become words. Words become action. Actions become character. Character becomes destiny.
©2024 ThinkVirtues, LLC. All Rights Reserved.

ThinkVirtues®

REFLECTION

ThinkVirtues®

REFLECTION

_____

_____

_____

_____

_____

_____

_____

_____

_____

ThinkVirtues®

Thoughts become words. Words become action. Actions become character. Character becomes destiny.
©2024 ThinkVirtues, LLC. All Rights Reserved.

ThinkVirtues®

Respect

FOCUS 1

The Meaning of Respect

Respect is treating someone the way you would like to be treated. It shows that you value the other person and consider their feelings, interests, beliefs, and ideas. There is an element of respect that is extended to someone because they have earned it; honor is given, but respect is earned. You must extend respect to others as a means of earning their respect.

Respect can also include admiration for another person or their accomplishments. Even if you don't respect someone, you honor a person because of their position (a parent, teacher, boss, or older person) or their beliefs (religion or culture), so you treat them with courtesy. You also honor your country because it holds a high place in your heart and mind.

Respect can also be shown in how you treat the environment (recycling, reducing waste, conserving resources), personal space (your or others' bodies), or possessions (your or another's toys, furniture, property). This kind of respect is an extension of your respect for yourself and others in your life. You are more likely to respect others and their possessions when you respect yourself. Respect for the environment shows caring for the larger world while respect for personal space and possessions tends to show consideration for those in your immediate world.

Caring interactions between people can, over time, create and build mutual respect. When someone offers a different idea or opinion, instead of countering with your own ideas, you acknowledge what that person has offered before sharing your own thoughts. This requires careful listening in order to fully understand the other person, their ideas, and their viewpoint.

ThinkVirtues®

FOCUS 1

Respect can be shown by behaviors (opening doors, greeting a person, being polite, showing courtesy, listening), tone of voice (keeping voice at an appropriate level, not shouting), and language (avoiding foul language and sarcasm, using polite words, not interrupting).

Cultivating respect is a virtue that can be practiced in the home, at school/work, or in the larger community. By respecting a person, you treat them in a way that is appropriate and reflects kindness, courtesy, and acceptance.

What are three ways you can practice Respect?

1. _____

2. _____

3. _____

Thoughts become words. Words become action. Actions become character. Character becomes destiny.
©2024 ThinkVirtues, LLC. All Rights Reserved.

ThinkVirtues®

Respect
FOCUS 2

The Importance of Respect

Respect is another way of showing caring and of making the world a more pleasant place. Too often, people want respect for themselves but don't always offer it to other people.

When your children grow up, you want them to know their own value so that they respect themselves and others. This means that they don't allow disrespect to occur in their own words or behaviors, nor do they allow it from others towards them.

Sometimes, young teenagers engage in disrespectful behavior that is destructive and can even be fatal. If a person realizes she is not being respected, she needs to learn to disengage from an unhealthy relationship. Children and teens need to learn to show respect and be shown respect in return. In that way, they learn a strong sense of how they should and should not be treated in order to behave properly and know when to walk away if necessary; their parents won't always be there to tell them what to do.

Respect does not necessarily mean that you always agree with another person; rather, you can accept that your differences won't get in the way of your relationships, whether personal or professional. It also means behaving in such a way that you can work well together, despite those differences.

Mutual respect helps build a cooperative environment in which work is produced by using each other's ideas and including them so that the final result is richer, of better quality, and more thorough than what could be done with only one person's ideas. Collaborative relationships, built on mutual respect, foster more productive and positive interactions and accomplishments.

ThinkVirtues®

FOCUS 2

The Importance of Respect

Why is it important to practice Respect?

___

___

___

___

___

___

___

___

ThinkVirtues®

FOCUS 3

Visualizing and Meditating on Respect

Think of a time when someone showed respect to you. How did you know they respected you? What did it feel like to you? Was the respect mutual? Did you also show respect to them? What behaviors of yours showed respect?

Now think of a time when you felt disrespected. How did you know you were not respected? Was it a behavior, tone of voice, or language? Was the disrespect a response to your own disrespect? If so, what was your behavior, tone of voice, or language?

Now think of a person whom you highly respect. What inspires that respect? What has that person done to earn your respect? How do you behave when you are with that person? What behaviors and language demonstrate your respect for them?

Is there someone whom you don't respect? Why not? How could you build a foundation of respect with that person?

How have you shown respect for the environment? How does this help the world? What about respect for possessions or property? How does this help another person, even if you don't know the person involved?

_____

_____

_____

ThinkVirtues®

FOCUS 3

Visualizing and Meditating on Respect

ThinkVirtues®

Respect
FOCUS 3

Visualizing and Meditating on Respect

How will you invite and deeply embrace the essence of Respect?

_____

_____

_____

_____

_____

_____

_____

_____

_____

ThinkVirtues®

FOCUS 3

Visualizing and Meditating on Respect

How do you feel after you have succeeded?

___

___

___

___

___

___

___

___

VIRTUES IN ACTION - Empowering Kids and Families to Connect, Grow, and Thrive

ThinkVirtues®

Respect
FOCUS 4

Here are some books you will enjoy reading!
They show respect in the characters.
You can get these books from your local library or bookstore.

If you are 4 to 8 years old, you will enjoy reading:
Yoko by Rosemary Wells

How does the teacher help the children show respect toward different cultures? In what ways can you appreciate ethnic differences?

If you are 5 to 10 years old, you will enjoy reading:
Dear Children of the Earth by Schim Schimmel

How does Mother Earth ask for respect for herself and the animals? Write a letter from the point of view of an animal or plant on Earth asking for respect of their species. According to the story, what will happen to the Earth if respect is not shown to it?

If you are 6 to 12 years old, you will enjoy reading:
All I see is Part of Me by Chara M. Curtis

How are all things connected to each other in this world? How does unity lead to respect?

Thoughts become words. Words become action. Actions become character. Character becomes destiny.
©2024 ThinkVirtues, LLC. All Rights Reserved.

ThinkVirtues®

Respect
FOCUS 4

ThinkVirtues®

FOCUS 5

Let's be creative!

Create an artistic expression through pictures, words, movement, or music that demonstrates respect for a person(s). You can include respect for their possessions or property if that is appropriate. Include abstract aspects of respect such as feelings or responses. Begin your composition smaller, and then show how respect can build and increase over time.

Now create something showing your respect and care for the environment. Depict the contrast between not respecting the environment and respecting it. What are the consequences of each?

What words were used to represent both patience and impatience?

_____

_____

_____

_____

_____

ThinkVirtues®

FOCUS 5

Let's be creative!

Make a piece of art showing you practicing respect.

- **Write a story or drama**
- **Write a song or poetry**
- **Create a dance**
- **Make painting or drawing**
- **Create a collage**

You can use the space below or grab some fun materials.

Thoughts become words. Words become action. Actions become character. Character becomes destiny.
©2024 ThinkVirtues, LLC. All Rights Reserved.

ThinkVirtues®

Respect

FOCUS 6

Family Activity

Share your creative expressions with your family. As each person shares, listen carefully. Reflect back what you are seeing or hearing with statements such as, "So, you are saying that ___," or, "It sounds/looks like you are ____," or, "Could you please clarify what you meant by ____?" Continue listening until each person feels satisfied that their creativity has been understood and recognized for its worth.

After everyone has shared, talk about what it felt like. Was there respect for different ideas? Did anyone feel "put down" or disrespected? If so, why? How can you change that? What did it feel like when other family members listened so closely? How can a similar atmosphere of respect be created in each person's environment outside the home?

_____

_____

_____

_____

_____

ThinkVirtues®

FOCUS 6

Family Activity

How do you feel about this family activity?

ThinkVirtues®

Respect

FOCUS 7

Respect is sometimes one of those virtues that "I know it when I see it" but is hard to describe or put into words! Too often, it seems to be a one-way street – children should respect their parents, but parents forget to respect their children. Similarly, a young teen wants respect from peers and teachers but often doesn't show respect to the others in their world.

Respect works two ways. Parents showing respect for their children does not mean that they relinquish their responsibility to be parents, to guide and help their children learn and grow into responsible young people and adults.

Respecting children does mean listening to them and understanding that they have different ideas. It means respecting their personal space, and valuing and honoring them. It means loving them even when disappointed in their choices and behavior.

When it comes to discipline, respect means disciplining in such a way that retains the child's dignity and provides learning opportunities that are constructive and meaningful. Sometimes, it means acknowledging that adults, too, make mistakes and have to correct them. This serves as a model for how children can appropriately correct and learn from their mistakes.

Write down ways that you can create and develop respect for:

- Yourself
- Someone with whom you work as a colleague or peer
- Someone who is in a position over you such as a parent, teacher, or boss
- Someone who is much older than you
- Someone who is in a position under you such as a child, younger sibling, or employee
- The environment

ThinkVirtues®

FOCUS 7

ThinkVirtues®

Respect
REFLECTION

How do you feel when you are being respected? How do you feel when you do NOT feel respected? How do you assert yourself to express that you want and expect to be respected? Write down all the ways you will command respect in the universe.

___
___
___
___
___
___
___
___

ThinkVirtues®

REFLECTION

ThinkVirtues®

REFLECTION

Thoughts become words. Words become action. Actions become character. Character becomes destiny.
©2024 ThinkVirtues, LLC. All Rights Reserved.

ThinkVirtues®

REFLECTION

ThinkVirtues®

REFLECTION

ThinkVirtues®

REFLECTION

ThinkVirtues®

Thoughts become words. Words become action. Actions become character. Character becomes destiny.
©2024 ThinkVirtues, LLC. All Rights Reserved.

ThinkVirtues®

Thankfulness

FOCUS 1

The Meaning of Thankfulness

Thankfulness is a sense of appreciation for what a person has, both tangible and intangible. To practice thankfulness you must first become conscious of what you have for which to be thankful. Then comes a sense of appreciation for something you have (family and friends, a warm home, food), experiences (opportunities, vacations, health) or avoidance of a negative (an accident or other misfortune).

What are three ways you can practice Thankfulness?

1. _____

2. _____

3. _____

ThinkVirtues®

Thankfulness

FOCUS 1

Thankfulness

FOCUS 2

The Importance of Thankfulness

Cultivating a spirit of thankfulness results in better physical and emotional health and an overall sense of well-being. Generally, people who are thankful are happier and less likely to be depressed. Learning to be thankful for what we have tends to make us less likely to compare ourselves with someone who has more than we do. This then creates an ongoing, continuously thankful spirit that eliminates envy.

Thankfulness also often creates feelings of peace and contentment with one's life experiences and circumstances.

Why is it important to practice Thankfulness?

_____

_____

_____

_____

_____

ThinkVirtues®

FOCUS 2

The Importance of Thankfulness

ThinkVirtues®

Thankfulness

FOCUS 3

Visualizing and Meditating on Thankfulness

Close your eyes, and picture at least five things or experiences for which you are thankful. Picture yourself applauding enthusiastically for them, smiling, and celebrating each one. Imagine others joining in with thunderous applause over each selection. Keep your eyes closed, and notice if you find yourself smiling. If so, celebrate and be thankful for that! If not, deliberately smile as you review what you are imagining. Allow at least ten minutes to focus on your mental images, and allow your imagination to wander into other areas for which you are thankful.

How does this make you feel? Give this feeling a color and a place.

_____

_____

_____

_____

_____

_____

ThinkVirtues®

FOCUS 3

Visualizing and Meditating on Thankfulness

How will you invite and deeply embrace the essence of Thankfulness?

_____

_____

_____

_____

How do you feel after you have succeeded?

_____

_____

_____

_____

ThinkVirtues®

Thankfulness

FOCUS 4

Here are some books you will enjoy reading!
They show respect in the characters.
You can get these books from your local library or bookstore.

If you are 4 to 8 years old, you will enjoy reading:
Sylvester and the Magic Pebble by William Steig

What is the real magic in this story?

If you are 6 to 12 years old, you will enjoy reading:
The Giving Tree by Shel Silverstein

*Why does the tree not ask for anything in return
every time she gives something to the boy?
Do you think the boy is thankful to the tree? Why or Why not?
Which character would you like to be? The Tree or the Boy. Why?*

_____

_____

_____

ThinkVirtues®

Thankfulness

FOCUS 4

Thankfulness

FOCUS 5

Let's be creative!

Select five things for which you are most thankful. Using the medium of your choice, create something that illustrates those items or experiences. Your artistic expression doesn't have to be a perfect illustration. Rather, focus on the feelings of thankfulness and put those into your creation.

Use your experiences as your guide.

_____

_____

_____

_____

_____

_____

_____

ThinkVirtues®

Thankfulness

FOCUS 5

Let's be creative!

Make a piece of art showing you practicing thankfulness.

- **Write a story or drama**
- **Write a song or poetry**
- **Create a dance**
- **Make painting or drawing**
- **Create a collage**

You can use the space below or grab some fun materials.

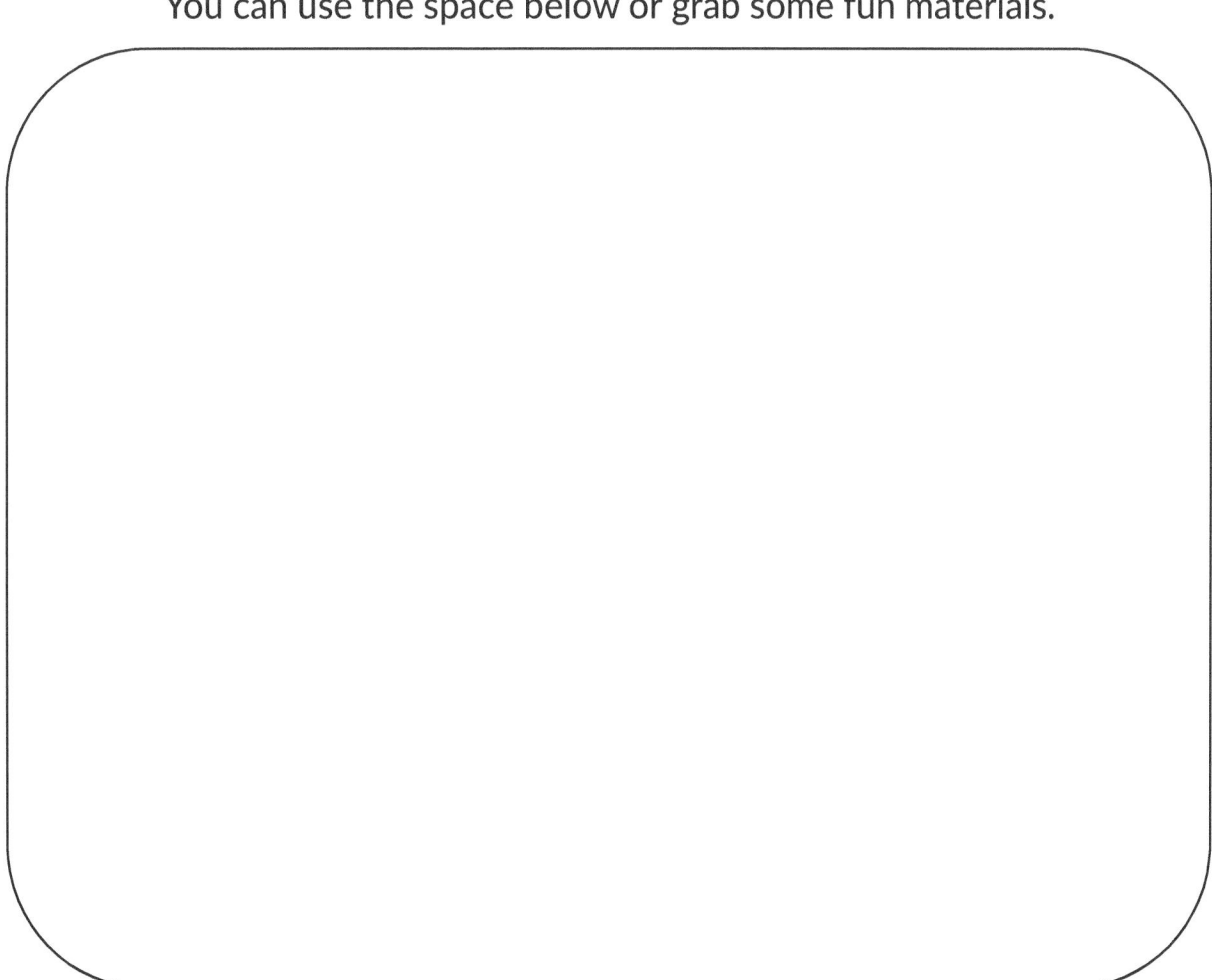

ThinkVirtues®

Thankfulness

FOCUS 6

Family Activity

As a family, create a chart of all the things for which each member is thankful. Have each person start with 5-10 items on the chart; then, place the chart in a prominent place in the home, and ask family members to add at least one thing to the lists each day of the week for at least two weeks, but preferably for a month.

Remember that thankfulness can be cultivated; in other words, deliberately focusing on those things for which a person is thankful tends to make the person more thankful. Remember that these could be "little" things (fresh water, clean clothes, sunshine, strength to get through a tiring day, a good night's sleep, children's toys or books) as well as "bigger" things (meaningful work, a warm home, enough food for three meals a day, a vacation).

_____

_____

_____

_____

ThinkVirtues®

FOCUS 6

Family Activity

How do you feel about this family activity?

___

ThinkVirtues®

Thankfulness

FOCUS 7

Stop to once again think about the things for which you are thankful that you visualized and/or created this week. Reiterate those items by writing a sentence for each one using the following format: I feel especially thankful for _____ because _____. After spending time in reflecting and writing your responses, share three of your "thankfulness" items with the family. If someone says something from your list, try to think of something different so that there are more thankful choices instead of everyone in the family naming the same thing(s). Remind each other to add to the Thankfulness chart you created during Focus 5, and tell each person how thankful you are that they are willing to celebrate thankfulness with one another each day!

_____

_____

_____

_____

_____

_____

ThinkVirtues®

Thankfulness

FOCUS 7

ThinkVirtues®

Thankfulness

REFLECTION

What are you most thankful for? How does being thankful make you feel? Take the time and reflect and write down in these next few pages all the things in your life your thankful for.

___

___

___

___

___

___

___

___

ThinkVirtues®

Thankfulness

REFLECTION

ThinkVirtues®

Thankfulness

REFLECTION

_____

_____

_____

_____

_____

_____

_____

_____

_____

ThinkVirtues®

Thankfulness

REFLECTION

ThinkVirtues®

Thankfulness

REFLECTION

ThinkVirtues®

Thankfulness

REFLECTION

_____

_____

_____

_____

_____

_____

_____

_____

_____

_____

ABOUT THE AUTHOR

Kathy Motlagh, CEO of ThinkVirtues, seeks to transform homes, educational communities and corporate environments into places where virtues thrive. Virtues, our 'mind muscles' as she calls them, are inherent in all of us. But they need to be learned, practiced and habituated, in order for humans to thrive. She has worked with many psychiatrists, social workers, and childhood education experts toward the development and implementation of the ThinkVirtues work and curricula.

Motlagh is an esteemed transformational coach and advisor to top CEO's and leaders globally. The proprietary framework and methods behind her unique, holistic, and transformational workshop, The Power of Authenticity, have been powerfully life- changing for most participants.

Motlagh helps her clients identify their top virtues. This critical step in advanced leadership mastery and development accelerates success and growth, both for individuals and within corporations. Motlagh empowers people to step into their authentic power and to express their creativity and genius in a way that wasn't available to them ever before.

Motlagh is the writer and creative force behind the Eutopia book series and accompanying products. She also serves as one of ThinkVirtues' chief content creators, curriculum writers, speechwriters and workshop creators. Additionally, Motlagh has vast experience facilitating workshops and coaching educators, parents, and employees.

Motlagh's business experience includes more than twenty years in business and finance, as a trusted advisor where she managed millions of dollars for a variety of groups and individuals.

- continued

ThinkVirtues®

She is a John Maxwell Team trained and certified speaker, leadership trainer and coach and has facilitated many corporate workshops and learning sessions. She has the proven ability to work with employees from a variety of corporate environments and manifold industries.

A graduate of the Art Institute of Chicago, Motlagh has used her creative and innovative muscles to empower and transform culture within homes and organizations. She has also taught art at the Montessori Academy of North Hoffman for seventeen years, where she worked to help empower children, educators, and parents. She has been an active board member of the school since its inception more than twenty-five years ago. Motlagh is a regular attendee of the Neuroscience Convention as well as an avid follower and researcher of psychiatry, physics, psychology and the social sciences, focusing on facilitating meaningful growth and transformational positive change.

Motlagh resides in Chicago and involves her family, including her two sons, in community service for local nonprofits and charitable causes.

ThinkVirtues®

ThinkVirtues®

VIRTUES IN ACTION FOR KIDS AND THEIR FAMILIES
A SERIES OF 6 BOOKS

The Virtues included in this book (BOOK ONE) are in **bold**.
The Master Collection Workbook includes all 55 Virtues.

Assertiveness	**Generosity**	Obedience
Caring	Gentleness	Orderliness
Cleanliness	Grace	**Patience**
Commitment	Helpfulness	Peacefulness
Compassion	Honesty	Perseverance
Confidence	Honor	Purposefulness
Consideration	Hopefulness	**Respect**
Cooperation	Humility	Responsibility
Courage	Humor	Self Discipline
Courtesy	Idealism	Service
Creativity	Independence	Sincerity
Detachment	Integrity	Tact
Empathy	**Joyfulness**	**Thankfulness**
Enthusiasm	Justice	Tolerance
Excellence	Kindness	Trust
Flexibility	**Love**	Trustworthiness
Forgiveness	Loyalty	Understanding
Friendliness	Moderation	Unity
	Modesty	

This is Book One in a Six-Book Series by ThinkVirtues®
Find more Books and the Master Collection of Virtues
at ThinkVirtues.com

Thoughts become words. Words become action. Actions become character. Character becomes destiny.
©2024 ThinkVirtues, LLC. All Rights Reserved.

VIRTUES IN ACTION - Empowering Kids and Families to Connect, Grow, and Thrive

Thoughts become words. Words become action. Actions become character. Character becomes destiny.
©2024 ThinkVirtues, LLC. All Rights Reserved.

www.ingramcontent.com/pod-product-compliance
Lightning Source LLC
Chambersburg PA
CBHW061811290426
44110CB00026B/2848